Reflections

Reflections

Dr. Ashok T Chakravarthy

PARTRIDGE
A Penguin Random House Company

To order additional copies of this book, contact
Partridge India
000 800 10062 62
orders.india@partridgepublishing.com

www.partridgepublishing.com/india

CONTENTS

Nature and we 1
What a delight 2
Overcoming... 3
Now and then 4
The worldly divides 5
If everyone strives.. 6
Lo! What can I do.. 7
Once and for all 8
Are we not... 9
Imparting an aspect 10
Care now for their tomorrow 11
To ignore or neglect 12
The perpetual alliance.. 14
Think positive 15
Hope! One after the other.. 16
Awake now, at least 17
That's the way 18
Ruthless destiny.. 19
Unless the human instinct… 20
The refuge of eternal joy... 21
May the 22
The eclipsed past 23
Love begins with me 24
A non-violent world 25
The ideals of peace 26
Relation 27
The awakening.. 28
The recurrence 29
S u n s e t 30
Attitude 31
In await of 32
Fleeting moments 33
I have to be a poet... 34
Though different... 35

The innerself 36
The destined fight 37
Breaking silence 38
Dispirited...39
The yearning 40
P r o m i s e s...41
Gain wisdom 42
Agitate memories 43
The ultimate fear..44
The inner light 45
The snow..46
Human instinct 47
A poem for the life 48
Midst the silence..49
Enlightenment 50
The amalgamation 51
In quest of amity...52
Oh god! let me 53
The pursuit...54
If not 55
A sanctorum of peace..56
Betwixt delights..57
Let us say..58
The disorder 59
A source for refuge..60
Trauma and furore...61
T h e c o n f e s s i o n..62
Freak invasions..63
In await of a new dawn 64
Evasive instinct 65
Harmonious path...66
The barren scapes of solitude.......................................67
How can you 68
The marching time...69
Canonization 70
The parting 71
At whose behest 72
N i g h t m a r e..73
T h e b r e a c h..74

A promise forever 75
Break-even point 76
The thought of tomorrow 77
Charming night 78
Refuge 79
Urban psyche 80
Driving the pains out 81
When shall we awaken 82
Give "peace" another chance 83
M e r c y 84
When realism dawns 85
In the night pub 86
Torn apart 87
Midst illusions 88
Let's aspire to …… 89
A dream real 90
The light of wisdom 91
The barriers 92
No where to escape 93
Tomorrow seems …… 94
H u m i l i a t i o n 95
The travails 96
H a t r e d 97
Throw some light 98
Ever-new solace 99
Midst an exile 100
A poets' heart 101

**Prologue to the Poetry Book
'REFLECTIONS'
of Dr. T. Ashok Chakravarthy, D.Litt., India**

By : Prof. Dr. Ernesto Kahan, Israel

Dr. T. Ashok Chakravarthy, is a great Indian writer, essentially an international poet who inscribes his lyric in favor of universal peace and harmony. He is a Universal Peace Ambassador and the Vice-Chair, Global Harmony Association. For me he is part of a magnificent river. I dedicate to him the following verses which I wrote in 2011:

> The river arrived...
> Bringing water, sweet and in love -
> Transparent drops and ice from the mountains
> Mother Himalayas, mother Aconcagua...
> When it passed through India and Nepal,
> it is filled by meditation and compassion...

When he asked me to write a prologue for this book of his new poems, I felt much honored, and at the same time responsible. During all my life I have considered myself as a physician and a poet dedicated to tolerance, non-violence, peace, and alert about the threat of nuclear weapons as well as an emissary for the prevention of nuclear war.

I know Dr. T. Ashok Chakravarthy from many associations of writers and intellectuals for culture of peace and world harmony and from the World Congresses of Poets being organized by the World Academy of Arts and Culture. Although we communicate with each other in English, which is not my native tongue, we also know how to communicate in another, maybe more important language i.e., the language of the eyes and mind. In his poem entitled IMPARTING AN ASPECT he writes the following:

[...] The little human eyes
Can shower a sea of sorrow,
The little heart
Can hold an ocean of emotion;
They knows no language
Yet they can react and respond,
They have no barriers
Yet they see something beyond. [...]

This book is well integrated and flows from one poem to the following and in total is a hymn to nature, freedom, happiness and life:

[...] When the doors of nature in the universe
Were wide open with a pleasant view,
We, with selfish motives and ill-intention
Have let loose a reign of mass destruction [...]

[...] Blessed are the flowers which during nights blossom
Blessed are the buds which for a tomorrow dream,
Blessed are the clouds adorning the sky with delight
Blessed are we, whoever cherishes the adorable sight [...]

[...] Without love ....
    there is no tolerance
Without tolerance ....
    there is no peace
Without peace ....
    there is no prosperity
Without prosperity ....
    there is no happiness
Without happiness ....
    there is no meaning for life [...]

In the year 2009 I was commented that our current society is at a transcendental crossroads. On one hand, the use of natural resources is very efficient, but on the other, that same use is endangering the continuity of life on our planet. On one hand, new technology and systems of intensive production permit us to obtain an elevation in the quality of life for all humanity, but on the other, new conflicts are threatening to use weapons of mass destruction, mainly atomic, and with it the potential destruction of our civilization and life on Earth. Dr. T. Ashok Chakravarthy is clearly walking in the way of the protection of life and his poetry is highly enrolled towards that.

The author assumed a compromise in a beautiful manner and splendid lyric

> [...] Though ....
> Desperately I try to explore
> The prospects of meeting you;
> Destined, I anticipate
> Another cursed dawn
> Would dawn upon my sweet love.
>
> Tomorrow will definitely dawn
> But there cannot be another day
> Where memoirs can once again rejoice
> The sweetest delight of delights
> That is 'your memorable relation [...]

Reading this book and its fabulous poems, the readers feel also a compromise and want to walk together with the author

> [...] The nectar of love is the essence of peace
> It, in fact is life's eternal existence resource
> Both dwell within, yes, within all of us
> To savor the life's precious and memorable bliss [...]

Thanks to Dr. T. Ashok Chakravarthy for this brilliant book! I strongly recommend this book. ENJOY HIS POETRY!

- **Prof. Emeritus Dr. Ernesto Kahan MD**
- **University Professor - Poet – Physician, Tel Aviv University, Israel**
- **Honorary President of the Israeli Association Writers. Spanish Branch**
- **1st Vice President & Secretary General- World Academy of Arts and Culture USA**
- **Honorary President Co-Founder United Nations of Letters**
- **Vice President Intl Forum for Literature and Culture of Peace (IFLAC)**

A MARVEL OF POETIC 'REFLECTIONS'
A Foreword by Prof. Kodanda Ram
to Dr. Ashok T Chakravarthy's poetry collection

It passes my comprehension how human beings, be they ever so experienced and able, can delight in depriving other human beings of that precious right of freedom

... Mahatma Gandhi

When oppression and suppression of freedom and speech is imposed by force, the hushed-up feelings emerge out in the form of verse or couplet. Ultimately reaching the silent shores, such expressions travel and flow on the lyrical waves and free themselves from the tangle of suppression of freedom-seeking thoughts. Once softened, they emerge out in the form of beautiful and stirring couplets or verse. It is to proclaim with pride that the six-decade long struggle for Telangana statehood gave birth to several such writings by writers, singers, lyricists and balladeers in the Telangana region. And, through their writings and songs, these artists played a vital role in educating the masses and successfully advocating the dire need for fulfillment of the long-cherished cause. Dr. Ashok Chakravarthy is one such poet hailing from Hyderabad, the capital city of the newly formed (on 2nd June, 2014) Telangana State of India. Familiar for his poetic skills which brought him immense name and fame in the international arena of poetry, I too got deeply fascinated with his idiomatic ways of expressing things through poetry compositions. I feel it a great privilege to be a part and parcel of his fifth volume of poetry, titled, '**Reflections**'.

Having read poem after poem, the splendor of the expressions rhythmically unfold and drag the reader to the domain of peace and solace. Knitting poetry with the elements of universal peace, environment protection, children welfare, poverty and concern for nature; the poet weaves a spell with heart-pleasing words and phrases. Breaking the barriers of borders, religion and region, the poet imparts poetic message through his poems. The pretty lines in the poem, '**What A Delight**' .... *Amity and identity adorn the earth as ornamental peace / A place, where human love and concern should thrive; / Why can't we exhibit our wit, patience and tolerance? / To sort out forced alienations and budding differences ...* espouse in the reader the feelings of solace and serenity. His profound expressions in the poem '**Now And Then**' brings before our eyes the images of what poverty is and land our hearts in the vortex of emotion ... *With tattered clothes / I sight a child, / Perhaps an orphan / Who still reflect / At this mid-life / In my heart's eye.*

In a bid to spread the message of harmony and human co-existence, the poet proves his credentials as a *Universal Peace Ambassador* by creating the lovely poetic breeze that would prevail in a peace-filled world. This particular poem, '**A Non-violent World**' stands a testimony of the poet's peace yearning .... *When the waves of true love and emotion surge / Perfect Peace and contentment would resurge, / By helping the starving and serving the needful / A person is bound to reach a refuge of joy-eternal.* The mind-boggling rhyming and timing, exploring ever-new and beneficial messages through fragrance of love, allied with philosophical touch pleases the reader's heart. One such remarkable poem, '**Love Begins With Me**' ... *Naked, we come into the world, naked we would leave / But the one eternal thing that remains forever is, 'Love', / Like the buzzing bee swirling around the lotus-petals / We humans should encircle humanity, like love-pearls...* speaks as to how the theme enlightens and implants in us the seed of what the ultimate of life is!

The spiritual instinct in the poet surges and emerges out to poetically express the remarkably hidden thoughts of '*salvation through enlightenment*'. Thus flow the garland of words in the poem '***Enlightenment***' ... *Seek the light of Peace / To share the ultimate of passion / Seek the path of passion / To discover a source for salvation.* Further, a treasure of words flow from the poet's pen and a flock of feelings surround the poet's swarming thoughts. Gifted by these rare features, the poet communicates his emotive feelings through the poem '***The Pursuit***' with these pleasant lines ... *Though am alone, I had many a companion / With the beautiful nature around to fascinate / The poetic musings often stir around and oscillate / Scribbling one after the other solitary tune thereon.* Not lagging behind any poet in expression of excellent passionate feelings, the poem '***If Not...***' reflects the innate feelings ... *In memory of death-defying love, I hauntingly hurl / A feast of romantic poetry is bound to unravel / Lo! She has painted my life and its destination / If not, I cannot be a poet wielding the romantic pen.*

Almost all the poems in the prestigious collection, titled, **REFLECTIONS** possess a philosophical melody and at times they seem to be reaching beyond normal imaginations. Every line expresses a deep feeling, wherein dwells sensitivity and exemplary qualities that make a real poet. With a firm resolve if the readers aspire to understand the poems in a true spirit, they are bound to experience a spectacular lyrical and poetical delight.

I personally wish and advise all poetry readers and literary lovers to acquaint with this rare quality of writings presented through this brilliant compilation of poems. I wish Dr. Ashok Chakravarthy, all the very best in his future endeavors.

Prof. M. Kodanda Ram
Prof. of Political Science
Osmania University
Hyderabad – 500 007
Telangana State, INDIA

MS. SUSANA ROBERTS
e-mail : roberts_susana@hotmail.com
POET/WRITER-ARGENTINA
Dr Honoris Causa WAAC-2009
Vice Dir Iflac Argentina and Sudamerica
Ambassador of Peace-Genevre-Suisse
Honorary President Hispan American union writer
Honoray Member Global Harmony Association
Member Ethical Ecological World Assembly
Member Presidium World Forum -
Spiritual Culture-Astana_Kazajastan

A FOREWORD to 'REFLECTIONS'

(A collection of poems by Dr. Tholana Ashok Chakravarthy, Poet, India)

This wonderful collection of nearly one hundred poems are directed to question the current situation how humanity has been evolved from the most important point: its essence. This book is the outcome to help the devastated society lacking in values and the author intends, through poetic words illuminate the readers with such **Reflections**. This seems to be the propose of this writer, whose book is a warning to the whole society, a book full of universal meaning from the headline to the end, intense words accompany us.... *let us act perfect for a perfect future* (Nature And Me).

The poet declares about himself: to have been a poet: *"the prisoner of thoughts in the heart"* (Poet's heart) and from there he opens the awakening of consciousness from where one would go on uninterruptedly through the contents of poems in this great work. He also denounces and warns about situations of today, at the same time educates with advises. In the poem "Attitude", he says: *to safeguard the human instinct ... we have to change it ... we have to transform it ... we have to struggle for it,* and as a plea he says: *let us all understand human values .. let us all stand together with a sole aim... and* insists...*if everyone strives..if everyone.*

In the XXI century, we should have been advanced in spiritual goodwill with many solid bases in different parts of the planet, but it happens the opposite, so this author as a responsible contemporary intellectual in his worthy job; struggles for unity and brotherhood, solidarity and awakening of consciousness. This is a fact. There is something precious to recollect and recover which is allowing us to move forward towards universal progress with dignified human values. This author is a fountain of good inspiration to others, whether near or far from every faith. His words come from a pure poetic spirit nurturing co-existence and this is the moment for the people to live in peace with neighbors, and these precious feelings are meant for everyone's happiness.

We all have to stop, - to see, feel, listen each poem; listen with the heart as to what is happening all around and how we can overcome the adversaries. As the fact of being alive here and now, the presentation of poems provide an unparalleled delight, achieving a sense of introspection amongst the readers.

It is a great honor for me to write words about the work of an author like Dr. T. Ashok Chakravarthy, whom I fully admire, who lives far off from my country (Argentina), where different language, traditions and customs exist. But I agree with the concept of universal peace with universal action - building bridges of understanding with spiritual values without differences of any kind. The fight through poetry is demonstrated by him at the time he takes a pen and writes word after word from the true human soul - with love for humanity. In this way, the poet chose to make it possible to convey mankind the required patience and thought to survive inside a global technological growth with PEACE.

Reading Chakravarthy's poems hailing from the land of Spiritual India and of Mahatma Gandhi, unfold before me a complete bright view of an 'Indian's Universe' over this vast southern deserted place of wind (Argentina) and I realize that the goodness of this author illuminates every horizon. He says: let's *show our unity, overcome egoism, ideals of peace... in addition, love,* he is sensitive to the nature and mother earth *...does not neglect... with wounds all over / and the lurking shadows of devastation / look at us, mournful, pitiful and disgraceful, with a deep feeling awake, can we continue .. at least now, oh humans!*

As a reputed and universal admirable poet and writer, Dr. Ashok Chakravarthy is responsible for the great awareness of this time, which is resonating like an eternal song here in Occident and there in Orient. He says: *memory is my companion, it speaks any language.* Here, the poetic soul thrives within him without any blocks of walls and doors, but with words surging alive between the alternate reality of today, - a fresh look lost in a world that is emerging in small human stature with an invisible preaching to the eyes and mind. This is the important fact that prevails and this book (REFLECTIONS) is a good tool for the concretization for the next future that awaits us all.

Ms. Susana Roberts
e-mail : roberts_susana@hotmail.com
POET-WRITER-ARGENTINA

Dr. Leo Semashko
President : Global Harmony Association
(with 500 co-authors from 56 countries and in 17 languages)
State Councillor of St. Petersburg,
Philosopher, Sociologist and Peacemaker
Director: Tetrasociology Public Institute, Russia

FOREWORD TO DR. T. ASHOK CHAKRAVARTHY'S
FIFTH COLLECTION OF POEMS TITLED, REFLECTIONS

"This collection of poems 'REFLECTIONS' focuses on four main themes: peace, children, love and harmony. These poems inspire the reader. One feels that they are written by a poet who is deeply devoted to them. In fact, Dr. Tholana Chakravarthy is the Vice President of Global Harmony Association (GHA), and has published many brilliant poems about peace, harmony, and children on the GHA website "Peace from Harmony" (www.peacefromharmony.org) and in many books of GHA: *Global Civilization* (2009), *The ABC of Harmony* (2012), *Global Peace Science from Harmony*, etc.

Deep social responsibility of the poet-author is expressed in his words that we are helpless in the global horror of terror, because "we fail to co-exist in harmony" (poem THE DISORDER). He is confident that the way out of this horror lies only on a harmonious path (poem HARMONIOUS PATH). Unfortunately, this key idea does not find development in collection. But despite this, it wakes up the good feelings, draws the reader towards peace, love and harmony, reinforcing people, especially the youth, with faith and enthusiasm in them. It is very important for the spiritual progress of humanity. Therefore, I advise all readers, especially the young, closely acquainted with this collection of original poetry."

- Dr. Leo Semashko, President,
Global Harmony Association,
Address: 7/4-42 Ho-Shi-Min Street,
St. Petersburg 194356, Russia

Dr. Krishna Guranathrao
Kulkarni
Retd. Prof / Freelance Journalist

H.No. 35, 1ˢᵗ Cross
Rajaji Nagar, Behind Travel
Inn.
<u>*SATTUR 580 009*</u>
DHARWAD
KARNATAKA STATE

<u>FOREWORD</u>

"REFLECTIONS",   is the   second anthology out of the five collections I have read, enjoyed and contemplated by me, which is composed by a young friend of mine who is a   quadragenarian called Dr. Tholana   Ashok Chakravarthy, Litt.D, serving   as a Manager of well-known agricultural bank, named *"The Telangana State   Co-operative Apex Bank Ltd."* (TSCAB) having its Head Quarters in the Charminar-famed city of Hyderabad.

This anthology is a compilation of one short of hundred poems (Ninety Nine) which are all perfect lyrical poems. In this collection of poems the poet's **lyricism, imagination, mode of expression** and **emotion,** have found a relief in a joyous outburst of spontaneous expression.

It is an admitted fact that the study of such poems will certainly help the reader to enjoy the beauty of the expressions of those thoughts. Till today I got an opportunity of reading nearly 200 such elegant poems composed by the peace loving poet Dr. Tholana. I confess cogently that every poem of him has added a **millimeter** to my mental horizon.

I am of the firm opinion that Dr. Ashoka is a man gifted with great poetic talent and powers. He composes his poems as **ebulliently** as a great poet. As a poet he is enormously popular not only in India but also abroad. The chief quality of this great poet is his sincerity both in his life and in his poetry. In short simplicity is the core of his lifestyle. Simplicity is also the characteristic feature of a good poetry. I personally like his **robust simplicity, veracity** and **directness of concept**. No doubt he is a poet of **first water**.

Being a lyrist the poet has used the English language with **mastery and music**. There is the wealth and variety of vocabulary and poetic expression in his poetry. As there is a magic of enchantment in his songs, his lyrics have a sweetness and poignancy all their own. So it appears to the reader that they sing themselves into the universal heart. He is able to do by means of words what the musicians does by the meter and the painter does by means of colours.   The following lines of the poet upheld the remarks made above –

<u>In his poems sound and sense are inseparable</u> :
1. To break the trust,
   To bridge the trust,
   Which one is easier,
   Unhesitantly the first – (Break-Even Point)

<u>There is a slight variety in the rhythm of his poetry</u>:
2. Why can't we be apart in restoring "Peace"
   To make our planet Earth, "A SANCTUARY OF PEACE" -
   (A Sanctuary of Peace)

<u>He uses words for the sake of their sound effects</u> :
3. At midnight under the moon light
   I stand beneath with a drowsy delight – (When Shall We Awaken)

The poet is gifted with remarkable power of **speech**. While reading his poems one will notice the importance given by him for **communication** in his poems. He writes not for his own pleasure but primarily to communicate his own thoughts and emotions to his readers. That's why his poems are full of **messages:-**

<u>In this stanza the clarion call of the poet is sounded to awaken the people from a state of stupor</u>:
1. The Mother Earth with wounds all over ,
   And the lurking shadows of devastation,
   Looks at us, mournful, painful and disgraceful,
   Can we Awake now at least, O Humans ! - (Awake Now At Least)

<u>Plain familiar words in their natural order form the bed-rock of his style</u>:
2. Like buzzing bee swirling around the lotus-petals
   We humans should encircle humanity, like love pearls. – (Love begins with me)

<u>The philosophy of this couplet is that forgetfulness of our duty results from self indulgence</u> :
3. Let us be perfect for a future perfect,
   In a perfect way for a perfect world-   (Nature And We)

The poet is a **hero** by virtue of the fact that he reveals truth to us. He has a direct insight into reality. That's why; he is able to describe reality so vividly to us. The below mentioned lines go to prove this statement.

This couplet reveals complete understanding of human psychology:

1. Though I desperately try to break this silence ,
   I find no one near to grab the fleeing chance – (Lo! What Can I Do)

There is the flow of rhythm and brevity of expression:

2. Unless the Sun sets there won't exist an iota of life ,
   Yes, let us think positive and brave the paths of grief – (Think Positive)

His poetic diction is mostly simple and clear:

3. Lo! Where are we heading to haunts me often ,
   Encircled by ecological break and crying orphans. -
   (The Disorder)

Dr. Chakravarthy is a poet of **nature**. He loves nature and worships nature .Like Wordsworth he loves nature as he finds it. He describes nature with admirable simplicity .There are several graphic descriptions of nature in this anthology. He laments for the exploitation of this good Earth. He criticizes this selfish tendency of man in his poems through soft words and in a milder way. To quote his own lines :

He describes vividly the nature of the exploitation of man in this stanza:

1. When the doors of nature in the universe ,
   Were wide open with a pleasant view,
   We with selfish motives and ill intention,
   Have let loose a reign of mass destruction – (Nature And We)
   No aspect of the activities of nature remains hidden from his searching eye:

2. The moon and stars are duty bound to enthrall ,
   Nature performs its task to help human survival – (Think Positive)

Thus nature seemed to him also divine, unspeakable deep as high as heaven.

The poet describes the pathetic conditions of the **poor** very minutely but it is with a more moving sympathy, a deeper pathos and brilliance of phrase. This pitiable plight of the poor has been depicted by the poet in these lines –

He paints the pitiable condition of the poor exactly as it is :

1. The hour after hour pounce ;
   Of the dreadful hunger
   Spreading its fatal tentacles,
   Deep in to poverty-stricken slums -   (How Can You)

<u>There is in him an eye to see and soul to do:</u>
2. Hunted by death trampled by hunger
   Poverty knocks the tolerance of the poor,
   Where do the strings of Mercy dwell? -   (Mercy)

The poet is a **propagator** of world peace. He gives much importance and priority for the maintenance of world peace in his poems. The following lines of the poet deserve to be quoted here :

1. On the ripples of freedom , float the thoughts of peace,
   Devoted! Let us honour and strengthen the ideals of peace
   - (The Ideals Of Peace)

2. Peace has become a distant mirage ,
   Unmasking violence with a fit of rage – (The Moments)

3. Lo! The so called protectors of peace ,
   Why not the wars could be averted - (A Sanctuary of Peace)

In almost all the poems of this **Anthology** the poet has expressed his unique emotional experience which is really a source of pleasure for the reader. To put the point in clear terms he sublimates emotions and offers aesthetic pleasures to the readers. So his poems have rather the value of a piece of creative literature than of mere emotions. He possesses a direct insight into reality . That's why he is able to describe reality so vividly to us .

In fine "REFLECTIONS", is a collection of short poems which set the readers imagination **ablaze** with lyrical fragrance. His poems are all realistic which serve as the **yardstick** to measure poetic talent. Moreover these short poems of him definitely reveal that he has a redefined and charming soul, a noble and amicable nature. Those who read his poems with devotion will certainly praise the qualities of his head and **heart**. What I observed and found in his poems is that realism does not   lie in the themes of his poems whereas it has been brought out through his magic of writing. He has expressed in his poems a noble **Philosophy** and it is the study of that philosophy that one should read this collection of poems, with a **seeing eye** and an **understanding eye**.

I personally feel proud that I got an opportunity to express my sincere opinions about the poetry of Dr. T. Ashok Chakravarthy in the form of a FORWARD to his collections of poems entitled, "**REFLECTIONS**".

I think that I am really BLESSED !

- **Dr. K. G. Kulkarni**
e-mail: kgkgadag@yahoo.com

NATURE AND WE

When the doors of nature in the universe
Were wide open with a pleasant view,
We, with selfish motives and ill-intention
Have let loose a reign of mass destruction.

Having pounded the surface and sea,
Having punctured the sky and space,
Having destructed the dense forests,
Having encroached the high mountains;

We have peeled natures' unbound beauty
We have devastated invaluable resources,
We have polluted the life-giving air,
We have spoilt the pure water resources.

We have invaded all living species,
We have infiltrated the green valleys,
We have played havoc with rare birds,
We have hunted down the rarest animals.

We have almost inflicted a death blow,
Dear! Yet some hope exists even now,
Ignorance of any sort at this juncture
Will turn the tide against the universe.

With perfect care and perfect concern,
With perfect word and perfect action,
Let us act perfect, for a future perfect
In a perfect way for a perfect world.

WHAT A DELIGHT

Autumn leaves flutter with the early morning gales
Dew drops sparkle under the reflecting sunrays,
The golden horizon unfolds another dawn, delightful
Soft and cool, a dream unfurls in thoughts castle.

Blessed are the flowers which during nights blossom
Blessed are the buds which for a tomorrow dream,
Blessed are the clouds adorning the sky with delight
Blessed are we, whoever cherishes the adorable sight.

Amity and identity adorn the earth as ornamental peace
A place, where human love and concern should thrive;
Why can't we exhibit our wit, patience and tolerance?
To sort out forced alienations and budding differences.

The sprouts of evil,-'injustice and non-cooperation',
The hassles of progress, - 'hatred, ego and rebellion',
When these are conquered with love and self-realization,
The planet earth is bound to become an abode of heaven.

Instead of ruin, we foresee equivalence and prosperity
Instead of darkness, we shall see a worthwhile future;
The clouds of passion shall shower everlasting trust,
The winds of change shall blow every atom of mistrust.

On the ripples of freedom, float the thoughts of peace
What a delight, if we pledge for such a worthy cause!

OVERCOMING...

Basing on the element of human 'love'
Overcoming selfishness, let's stand high above
Basing on the element of human 'identity'
Overcoming egoistic attitude, let's show our unity
Basing on the element of 'equivalence'
Overcoming partiality, let's show no difference
Basing on the element of 'justice'
Overcoming injustice, let's fight without truce
Basing on the element of 'friendship'
Overcoming enmity, let's create a fair relationship
Basing on the element of 'cooperation'
Overcoming all hassles, let's choose a real action.

Move! Shouldering a compassionate responsibility
Let's ensure, there won't be betrayal of equality;
Protecting the present, laying the paths for future
Let's ensure, coming generations feel more secure.
Our commitment should be to shun human 'alienation',
Our pledge should be, for 'connectedness and realization';
Only then, we all can enjoy the ever-new pleasing joy
To view, clouds of peace and freedom adorn the sky.

NOW AND THEN

The delights
Of childhood
Surge in me.
My elated mood
Gets submerged
In the warmth
Of childhood days.
My fondling mother
My loving father,
In their cozy arms
I feel wrapped
With joy infinite.
The very moment
I am forced out
Of the short trance;
I fall apart
For, at a cross road
With tattered clothes
I sight a child,
Perhaps an orphan
Who still reflect
At this mid-life
In my heart's eye.
Oh God!
Why such disparity?
Why such inferiority?
Where might be he!
Without food, and
Without a shelter;
Whose presence
Moved me
Even at childhood
And still keeps
Haunting me
Now and then.

THE WORLDLY DIVIDES

It's a most ill-fated day …
When everything went astray,
Breaking the bond of our 'love'
And pulling me from skies above;
The cradle of dreams, you broke,
And, on a thorny path I fell awake.

The cozy flowers of beauty
Which blossom as a routine duty;
Perhaps never bothered…
That, soon they shall fall withered,
Or may get forcibly plucked
And mercilessly thrown unnoticed.

Yes, the battle of life is hard to fight
Yet, for survival every life fights,
But, a lazy and thoughtless revolt
Creeps in me after the 'love jolt';
Yet, I am happy to breathe again
For in my heart, strongly you remain.

All the worldly divides can be broken
But, do not break the heart of a human,
It is a place where 'love' dwells
It's a source, where love speaks or tells;
Sacrificing pride, let's choose a path
That draws us close with eternal warmth.

IF EVERYONE STRIVES

Without love ....
    there is no tolerance
Without tolerance ....
    there is no peace
Without peace ....
    there is no prosperity
Without prosperity ....
    there is no happiness
Without happiness ....
    there is no meaning for life.

Through love blossoms peace,
    Which paves a way for prosperity,
Through prosperity blossoms happiness
    Which fulfills everything we aspire,
These are the four strong pillars
    On which our 'lives' can build progress;
These are the four strong options
    On which our 'future' can solidly rely,
These are the four strong spheres
    In which we ought to 'stand united'.

Blessed, blessed will be humans
    If everyone strives for universal welfare;
Stability and integrity, if gets endangered
    The principles of freedom get ditched,
And, the driving force that lifts us all
    Is unity that breaks all cobwebs of despair,
And, the fruits of peace will be within reach
    Once we see our fondest hope blossoming.

LO! WHAT CAN I DO

The night spreads a carpet of darkness
Over the far off hillock, the moon rises,
The eerie silence is intermittently broken
By the barking dogs, somewhere hidden.

The life supposed to dawn by tomorrow
Would it alter the current phase of sorrow?
The emotionally-laden, fearful stalking heart
Longs to evade this trauma at every sunset.

The same life, the same stream of feelings
Keeps moving, faltering yet steadily moving;
Lighting a lamp, I draw my old pen and book
Peeping through the small window to jot a lyric.

The orphaned and the starving street children
Influence my thoughts with a wave of emotion,
My mind gets blocked with a veil of dejection,
Lo! What can I do, rejected and left all alone.

When mind is ruled by thoughts of desperation
Who can but salvage the vanishing aspirations?
Like a little drop of water on a calladium leaf
Everything slips in a moment, except for grief.

Though I desperately try to break this silence
I find no one near to grab the fleeing chance.

ONCE AND FOR ALL

Memory is my companion
It speaks any language.
It knows extremely well
What with I am acquainted to.
While hopes keep on inspiring
And Illusions keep on motivating,
In search of emotional peace
I keep searching, but, all in vain.
The nature I utmost loved
The roses I most cherished,
The birds I sweetly watched
Whirl on my mind's screen.
The plundered days of past
The baffled years of youth,
And the tearful adieu you bid
Ruined every future path I laid.
Now, I can either speak of today
Or can speak about the tomorrow,
Under the debris of love-realm
The world of mine lay crumbled.
Except for the fast fading 'memory'
There is no reliable companion;
The eventual desire to reach you
Stands evaporated, once and for all.

ARE WE NOT

In the deep woods, stunning and beautiful
The black cuckoo sings a song, remorseful;
Concern on 'human-conflicts' it voices a tale
And the theme echoes across the hills and dale
Are we not co-living creatures on planet earth?

The caravan of black ants, run hither and thither
Infiltrations and invasions drive them with fear;
What if, if human-bond lives with self-acceptance
Lo! Love blossoms at any given time, at any place.
Are we not co-living creatures on planet earth?

A group of pigeons like a dangling cloud, flees
In the far-off habitats they hear human cries;
A mother for her child, a child for mother, weeps,
What with loathe and dispassion humans shall reap?
Are we not co-living creatures on planet earth?

The stream in the woods swarm with living creatures,
Without grudge they embrace diversity in all weathers;
But, they feel scared and insecure by human actions
They cannot express, yet enlighten us with reactions
Are we not co-living creatures on planet earth?

As a single sect of living creatures on the planet earth
Let's make a difference by sharing love and faith;
This universal bond is the essence of our survival
Let's ensure; buds of love begin to blossom in real.
And impart, we are co-living creatures on planet earth!

IMPARTING AN ASPECT

The little human eyes
Can shower a sea of sorrow,
The little heart
Can hold an ocean of emotion;
They knows no language
Yet they can react and respond,
They have no barriers
Yet they see something beyond.

The beauty of nature
They store in warm memories,
The colorful birds and animals
They store in memories annals.
Emotion or a burst of angst
Originates from these sources,
And, the waves of love and concern
Surge from unfathomable depths.

The heart may one day stop
The memories may forever erase,
But, the eyes have no instant death
For, they can gift their sight
To those deprived of eye-sight
Even after a human becomes lifeless.

Let us script this in memory
And throw light on giving sight
Which act is an act upright?
That not only can provide eye-sight
But a real meaning to human birth.
It's everyone's responsibility to impart
To impart this aspect to one and all.

CARE NOW FOR THEIR TOMORROW

A blanket of chillness wraps the moon-lit night
The otherwise busy city streets look isolate
It's almost calm except for occasional barking dogs,
The street lights look dim, midst the layers of fog.

A group of street children, perhaps rag pickers
Cover their dusty bodies with rubbish plastic papers;
Shivering with torn clothes, body sucked to the bone
They look almost lifeless, deserted by every human.

Their pathetic plight and inexplicable dejection
Alas! Fail to have an impact on human relation.
While wars and conflicts loom large, alarming,
With selfish objectives, yet, humans keep on vying.

Having become own victims of calamities and wars
Aware though, life is but a short-lived bubble in the air;
Humans, least concerned on sharing love & humanity,
Fight again and again for dictatorship & superiority.

On the desolate paths, fearsome and totally dark
Let our love & concern for children grow like a spark
Lest, we are going to spoil their future of tomorrow
Hence shower love on them & shatter their sorrow

Yes! Child trafficking, child abuse and child labor,
Unchecked are they growing in every nook and corner
Yes! Until the inhumane instinct is driven out
And, unless the egoistic attitude is shunted out
How can we protect the essential rights of children?
How can we promote the basic welfare of children?

TO IGNORE OR NEGLECT

The delights
Of childhood
Surge in me.
My elated mood
Gets submerged
In the warmth
Of childhood days.
My fondling mother
My loving father,
In their cozy arms
I felt wrapped
With joy infinite.
The very moment
I am forced out
Of the short trance;
I fell apart
For, at a cross road
With tattered clothes
I sight a child,
Perhaps an orphan
Who still reflect
At this mid-life
In my heart's eye.

Oh God!
Why such disparity?
Why such inferiority?
Where might be he!
Without food, and
Without a shelter;
Whose presence
Moved me
Even at childhood
And still keeps
Haunting me
Now and then.

Is there a scope but
To give priority to children
For their well-being and welfare
And, apart giving protection
To the basic rights of children.
Caringly and collectively
Together if we make a move
With a future vision, to ensure
There is no scope for humanity
To ignore or neglect children.

THE PERPETUAL ALLIANCE

No, we are not, we are not alone
Either you or I should never feel alone
Within us dwells a sweet soothing soul
A companion, an invisible force to console.

The constant view of roadside poverty
Get capsized within our emotive anxiety,
Helpless, inner self tries to be assertive
Forcing us to re-think and act positive.

The pains of those caught in such suffering
Tries to knot us with that distressful string
Feeling cornered, somehow we aspire to view
And feel elated for having such deep buried love.

A soul's concern for the blind and the orphans
Often awaken our inner self with new emotions,
For a while, we get carried in a thoughtful trance
But, mind tries to shrug it off with a quick glance.

Yes, heed to the truths unfurled by inner soul
To reckon the worldly reflections which are real;
We have to change our motto, bit by bit, at least
Do not forget, the perpetual alliance is our spirit.

THINK POSITIVE

The beautiful flowers have to wilt tonight
And pave a way for the new buds to sprout,
The hapless birds rush to hide with fright
To rejoice again at the knock of dawn, in await.

The pitiable sight of a bone sucked beggar
The pathetic plight of untimely death of a dear,
The emotionally charged heart of a jilted lover
Everyone dread the recycling trend of sunset hour.

The darkness which infiltrates through the sunset
The fiery instinct within, which peeps to gush out,
Prompt things to get astray, with uncertainty at hilt
Without giving scope to counter the chronic torment.

The moon and stars are duty-bound to enthrall,
Nature performs its task to help human survival,
Unless the sun sets, tomorrow cannot dawn here
Yes, act positive to dispel every gloom and fear;

Unless the sun sets there won't exist an iota of life
Yes, let's think positive and brave the paths of grief.

HOPE! ONE AFTER THE OTHER

The doors of love
Slammed in disbelief,
Forcing me to suffocate
In search of a way out.
The lone string of hope
That's you….
Finally left out of the blue
Leaving me astray
In a spell of gloomy memories.

Though ….
Desperately I try to explore
The prospects of meeting you;
Destined, I anticipate
Another cursed dawn
Would dawn upon my sweet love.
Tomorrow will definitely dawn
But there cannot be another day
Where memoirs can once again rejoice
The sweetest delight of delights
That is 'your memorable relation'

Though in vain ……
Hopes hope against all hopes
The ultimate one …….
Lurks at the doorstep
Of another fading hope.
To outwit this nightmarish hour
One after the other hope
Impatiently waits, but in vain,
Expecting a fortunate love-filled dawn.

AWAKE NOW, AT LEAST

Stranded, he keeps on gazing
Gazing at the moving public,
Passing vehicles and fleeting world.
It's a rebirth, if he opens his eyes
At all, if sleep envelopes him,
It's death that stares in his dreams.

The dumb tree that gives him a shade
Day and night, is his only shelter;
Though the tree cannot speak,
It perhaps understands his agony;
While its leaves wipe his tears
Its twigs paint them in colors.

The drifting clouds, there above
Become dark and aspire to burst out.
The emotions of human sufferings
They seem to gather from high skies,
Through the humankind friendly trees
To quench our thirst, spell after spell.

The care and concern of eco-friendly trees
We ignore, as we ignore a street beggar.
The Mother Earth, with wounds all over
And the lurking shadows of devastation
Looks at us, mournful, pitiful and disgraceful
Can we AWAKE now at least; O Humans!!

THAT'S THE WAY

As in the past
Tonight too, like me,
The city is fast asleep.
But, with me along
It too wakes up early
It moves, but I cannot.

At times,
It rains in torrents,
At times,
It stirs a wave
Of scorching heat,
At times,
It throws a blanket
Of bone-chilling cold.
Yet, everything moves on
Without any interruption.
That's the way of a city life.

Neighbors or others
Orphans or beggars,
Ignoring them as strangers
They live with selfish motives
To secure every comfort and joy.
No one cares for anyone
Confining love for their dear ones;
They make every move
To achieve their goal of lasting joys.

But, destiny imparts them
The ultimate of 'what life is',
Alas but, it is already too late
For they are crippled by age
And thirsting for love and refuge;
But who is there to listen,
It's a part and parcel of a city life.

RUTHLESS DESTINY

A renewed hope sprang
When the hours of dawn rang,
As usual, the dawning sun
Peeps through the glowing horizon.

Filling hearts with new delights
The birds of beauty fly out;
While the darkness fizzles out
They dispel all gloomy thoughts.

Today is but unimaginable
Tomorrow is yet unpredictable;
Fearing the outcome of today
I feel loving the bygone day.

The waning out life, in isolation
The mood of clouding dejection;
These moments cause torment
And chase me without a respite.

Down, I fall umpteen times,
Yet, manage to balance at times,
But, the reprieve I deeply seek
Evade me, giving a mystic slip.

The destructible human body
Is bound to worn out one day,
And, when life is in the ascending
Remember, everything looks peeling.

And, in the merciless hands of fate
Doomed, we become a tool of hate;
And, the invisible tentacles of destiny
Finally grab without an iota of mercy.

UNLESS THE HUMAN INSTINCT...

Unless the human instinct within is brought out,
Unless the egoistic attitude is discarded out,
How can the rights of children are protected?
How the welfare of children can be promoted?

A blanket of chillness decorate the night with isolation
The otherwise busy city streets look with desperation,
The street-lights look dim covered by layers of thick fog,
It's almost calm, except for occasional barking of dogs.

A group of street children, perhaps poor rag pickers
Cover their dust-laden bodies with rubbish papers;
Tottered clothes cover their sucked to bone bodies,
Almost lifeless they look, abandoned by human vagaries.

The thoughts of desperation, add to deep depression
Piercing their heart of hearts in a fit of aggression;
With selfish motives, humans have ignored all faiths
With wars and natural calamities torturing the earth.

On the desolate looking paths, scary and totally dark
Why not our concern for children glow like a spark,
Let us shower love on them and shatter their sorrow
To ensure the children to tread a bright path tomorrow.

THE REFUGE OF
ETERNAL JOY

By the merits of great good fortune
A human birth is we bestowed upon…..
Like jewels of crown in the kingdom of love
Let our god-gifted discriminate power glow.

The nectar of love and the essence of peace
In fact are life's eternal co-existence sources
Both dwell within, yes, within all of us
To savor life's precious and lasting bliss.

Lured by ever-luring worldly entanglements
We break the citadels of right conduct;
Clasping thorns of selfishness and riches
We assume them as fresh blooming roses.

Transient and destructible is what 'life' is
Yet, forfeiting true joy we run after mirages;
Discovered truth, we fling at vultures of desires
Preferring to survive on illusions and fantasies.

But, fulfillment of human birth as a precious one
If searched, is found in love and devotion;
Why should we invite the tormenting fissures?
Which push life betwixt the birth-death sphere.

When the waves of true love and emotion surge
Perfect happiness and contentment would resurge,
By helping the starving and serving the needful
One is bound to reach the refuge of joy-eternal.

MAY THE ....

May the hopes of dejection fade away
Wiping away all fears and hatred;
Sowing the seeds of love and faith
With concern and delight let us tread,
Tread the righteous and moral path
That unites and leads us to peace.

May the bond of love and concern
Towards co-humans remain forever,
And, let the pollution of hatred
Get totally ousted and destroyed.
And a solid eternal foundation
For a human-bond is laid forever.

May the lives of the down-trodden
Get uplifted by humane efforts,
May the uncertain lives of orphans
See a ray of hope and affection.
Let a glorious and spectacular future
Welcome them with open arms.

May this transient earthly life of ours,
By the positive thoughts of peace
Get purified inwardly and outwardly
And sow a spirit to valiantly resist
The ill-intended moves of betrayers
Who often play havoc with human lives!

THE ECLIPSED PAST

A long and steep gaze
Into the eclipsed past,
Provide my thoughts an edge
To unroll the bygone past.
Paths adorned with flowers
Became skyscraper blocks,
The playground glitters
Sans the delightful brook.
Childhood flew into teens
Joys became a scarce rainbow,
Age changed the directions
Flooding me in life's flow.
Some gripping circumstances,
Paved the way to widen distances;
Like the silent skyscrapers
I too stare into the hollow skies.
Agonized thoughts feel the stress
Exploring a shore or an ultimate?
Gripped by never-ending distress
Midst stark realities, I suffocate.
The very moment they learnt to fly
Birds flew away by the tempting age;
Searching an oasis, aloud I cry
Lo! Am I following a deceit mirage?
The steep gaze, the eclipsed past
Haunt without respite, day and night,
The city environs brim with delight
But many a life wipe out in this desert.

LOVE BEGINS WITH ME

With firmly rooted trust, implanted in every human
And, like lamp-bearers of 'Love'; if with us love begins,
The inexperienced delights, like waves of compassion
Gush out of human hearts and groom new human relations.

There shall neither be any scope for wars and conflicts
Or shall there exist scope for a volley of inhuman attacks,
In the warmth of 'Love', with deep concern for co-humans
Hatred and grudge, reduced to ash would be overthrow.

Naked, we come into the world, naked we would leave
But the one eternal thing that remains forever is, 'Love',
Like the buzzing bee swirling around the lotus-petals
We humans should encircle humanity, like love-pearls.

The whole of the world is a spectacle of mere illusions
Nobody belongs to anybody, yet, surely we are but one
Let this be the saying of humanity, like that of creation
The elixir of which is 'Love', where dwell all solutions.

If every human comes forward with a decisive thought
Saying, 'love begins with me', 'love begins with me',
Waves of surging love would dance in every human heart
Yelling, let us co-exist in every heart and in every part.

A NON-VIOLENT WORLD

The nectar of love is the essence of peace
It, in fact is life's eternal existence resource
Both dwell within, yes, within all of us
To savor the life's precious and memorable bliss.

But, lured by the materialistic worldly delights
We break the citadels of our right conduct;
Clasping the thorns of selfishness and riches
Under illusion, we assume them as cozy roses.

Transient and destructible is what a human 'life' is
Forfeiting true joy we run after non-existing peace;
Flinging pronounced truth at the vultures of desires
We prefer to survive on lost hopes and fantasies.

When the waves of true love and emotion surge
Perfect PEACE and contentment would resurge,
By helping the starving and serving the needful
A person is bound to reach a refuge of joy-eternal.

'The culture of peace' is a most treasurable one
It understands everything with love and concern;
We can eliminate destructions of war and hatred
And, we can definitely foresee a non-violent world.

THE IDEALS OF PEACE

Autumn leaves flutter with the early morning gales
Dew drops glitter under the reflective sunrays,
The golden horizon unfolds another dawn, delightful
The longing for peace unfurls in my thoughts castle.

Blessed are the flowers which during nights blossom
Blessed are the buds which for a tomorrow dream,
Blessed are the clouds adorning the sky every night
Blessed are we, whoever cherishes the adorable sight.

Faith and amity adorn the earth as ornaments of peace
A place to bask under the warmth of love-surging eyes;
Why can't we exhibit our wit, patience and tolerance?
To sort out roaring frictions and surging differences.

The sprouts of evil; 'hatred and egocentric ambitions',
The hassles of progress; 'injustice and non-cooperation',
When both are conquered with love and self-realization,
The planet earth is bound is become an abode of heaven.

Instead of ruin, we foresee equivalence and prosperity
Instead of darkness, we shall see a worthwhile future;
The clouds of passion shall shower everlasting trust,
The winds of change shall blow every atom of mistrust.

On the ripples of freedom, float the thoughts of peace
Devoted! Let us honor and strengthen the ideals of peace

RELATION

Alone! No, we can never be alone
Yes, you or I should never feel alone,
Within us dwells, yet another soul
A companion, invisible force to console.

The reflections of roadside poverty
Get captured within our emotive anxiety
Helpless, yet inner self tries to be assertive
Striking us to re-think, relatively positive.

The pains of those caught in suffering
Inner self aspires to knot us with that string
Feeling cornered, we somehow agree to its view
And feel elated for possessing such hidden love.

Yes, its concern for the blind and the orphans
Often awaken our innerself with emotions,
For a while, we get carried in a thoughtful trance
Yet, we try to shrug it off at the earliest glance.

Yes, heed to the truths unfurled by inner soul
To reckon the worldly reflections which are real
We have to change out motto, bit by bit at least
Don't forget, the perpetual alliance is our spirit.

THE AWAKENING

The soul itself is our lamp
One has to bask under its glow
Blow it not with greed and pride
Invoke not the paths of darkness.

The glow that encircles the universe
Is put at stake for some selfish ends
Peace has become a distant mirage
Unmasking violence with a fit of rage.

Starvation deaths on one side
Storming clouds of war on the other
In between these devastating storms
Innocent lives are forced to perish.

Trees and flowers of love lay uprooted
At the anvil of doomed human instinct,
Every moment has become unpredictable
Is it the beginning or end of a war-torn world?

Yes, awaken the devout wisdom in you
To take guard at the axis of peace and love
Be a person who serve the cause of many
But not a slave to the emotions and money.

THE RECURRENCE

The recurring memories
Like clouds of emotion
Surge out all of a sudden
From a volcano of musings.

The detracted dreams
Assemble in the irises of eyes,
Unfurling thoughtful realms
Desires flirt in search of joys.

The charming colorful world
The love-filled ecstatic waves
Embalm the bleeding wounds,
It's too late to undo the damage

Where do the musings emerge
Why do they strike in silence
Memories recur and blow like lava
Perhaps to stir yet another storm

SUNSET

The beautiful flowers have to wilt by tonight
To pave a way for the new buds to sprout
The hapless birds have to hide with fright
To rejoice again at dawn, lurking in await.

The pitiable sight of a bone sucked beggar
The pathetic plight of a fate-clinched son dear,
The emotionally charged heart of a jilted lover
All in all, dread the recycle of the sunset hour.

The darkness which infiltrate through the sunset
The fiery instinct which lurk to gush out
Prompt things to get astray, with uncertainty at hilt
Without any scope to counter the periodic torment.

But, apart from humans, nature has to survive
The moon and stars have to enthrall and thrive
Accustomed to hassles, destined are to grieve
That's how a sunsets, without regrets to bereave.

Unless the sun sets, tomorrow cannot dawn here
Yes, act positive to dispel the gloom and fears
Unless the sun sets, everything would be extinct
Yes, think positive to keep all the fears at rest.

ATTITUDE

An astrologer, long ago I met
Predicted what perplex me now
Of course, may also astound you.
He was courteous
He was generous
He was selfless
And fascinating to rely upon.

How could I conclude this
…. You may guess in askance.
Instead of reading my future
He foretold the prevailing evils
He foresaw the inhuman instinct
He expressed the plight of humans
Sad, devastating and dejecting.

Now, I presume…..
Something has to be done by all
To safeguard the human instinct
…. we have to change it
…. we have to transform it
….. we have to struggle for it
Let us all understand human values
Let us all stand together with a sole aim
To stem the changing trends
To nip off the changing attitude.

IN AWAIT OF ....

The doors of love slammed,
In disbelief
Forcing me to suffocate
In search of a way out.
Yes, the lone string of life
That's you
Finally left, snapped
Leaving astray
A volley of gloomy memories.

Though ....
Desperately I try to explore
The prospect of possessing you,
I suspect ....
Destiny will push another cursed dawn.
Yes, tomorrow will definitely dawn
But, hardly can there be another day
Where memories can rejoice
Unless you turn-up,
Against grim presumptions.

Though in vain ......
Hopes hope against each
The ultimate one ....
Lurks at the doorstep of expectancy
To outwit this nightmarish hour
Persisting in vain,
In await of a love-filled dawn.

FLEETING MOMENTS

Scattered by the stars in deep skies
The beauty of nature surround the night
The rotund moon is splendid and bright
Lo! The delight is worth a feast to eyes.

This night, like a routine night is different
…. perhaps lured by the gentle breeze …
Perhaps fascinated by the flowers of delight
It fascinates with an adoring view seize.

Carried by the fleeting and captivating thoughts
I slowly slip and surrender into the warm clasp,
The thoughts of ecstasy under the spell of delight
Like a firefly, whirl and drag me within its grasp.

The fleeting moments are bound to run ahead
The starry skies and the bewildering beauty too;
Yes, the present phase is temporarily surcharged
Under the spell youthful hearts kneel by its woo.

I HAVE TO BE A POET

Don't miss the opportunity, Look, look, look
See, how the high tides rush out of the shores
I would stagger in my words of expression
Lo! The beauty is a memorable feast to eyes.

Lo Sea! The clouds that adorn you quite often
The stars which cover you like a blanket, by dusk
Often draw my musings onto a heavenly abode
Aspiring to illustrate, whenever I tune to you.

Fortunate are those, who can judge you
A mere touch and embrace of your warm layer
Would definitely move any heart with thoughts
To stay away for a while, from the worldly hassles.

Yes, the time keeps fleeting
The waves too keep slashing
They break and break with a flash of beauty
O Sea! I know, time and tide wait for none.

Yes, memories do not fade till the exit time
For natures' sake at least, "I HAVE TO BE A Poet".

THOUGH DIFFERENT

Invisibly, we follow her gentle song
Swinging like a fresh flower, all along
She is the breeze, she is the craze, we long
No one would hesitate to sing a song along.

But, who can pour life to a frustrate orphan?
Who can provide succor to the starved lot?
Humiliated by the society with blind principles
What song can they prefer with an emotive tone.

Who would care whom, if doomed by poverty
Who would love whom, if love overflows ashore
Are those ignored be called doomed …..
Or those loved be called the lucky ones?

Ways and means of life vary, likewise thoughts
Fortune and misfortune, like two poles apart …
Swing the wind of life between doom and luck;
Though different, both fluctuate in between doom.

THE INNERSELF

The doors of passion slammed,
In disbelief
I am forced to suffocate,
Desperate to find a way out.
The lone string of life
That's your "love"
Finally got snapped
Raising a havoc-storm in heart.

Though ….
Desperately I try to explore
The prospect of possessing you
I suspect, destiny will play cruel.
Yes, tomorrow will definitely dawn
Hardly can there be another day
Where memories can rejoice you
Yes, if you fail to turn-up.
Though in vain ……
Hopes hope against each
The ultimate one …….
Lurks at the doorstep of expectancy
To outwit the nightmarish hour
…. in vain, speak the innerself.

THE DESTINED FIGHT

With wounds bleeding, heart tolerates the pain
Though in vain it try to escape from the clutches
The scars of the healing wounds recur often
Without you, how can I comply with life's march?

A single pebble can create a flutter in the pond,
If countless pebble of thoughts keep on tossing
The heart should bear the impact of the impound
But, where's the balm if storms keep on ravaging.

The trauma of haunting solitude on one part
The deep longing to possess you on the other;
Though the losing option has a strong undercurrent
Can the hopes desert me at this crucial juncture?

The intolerable pain invade my already pathetic life
Though the fading hopes fight to keep it at bay
But, had I not been mauled by this unabated strafe
With yet another hope perhaps, I would fight to stay.

BREAKING SILENCE

Silently I watch
Moment after moment
Slowly slip into eternity.

Silently I feel
The invisible layers of wind
Blow past into perpetuity.

Silently I glimpse
Tide after tide in the sea
Get swallowed by another tide.

Silently I glance
The delightful buds
Blossom by the passing of night.

And silently I aspire
To fly like a home-coming bird
Across the golden horizon of setting Sun

Yes, silently I dream
To experience the bountiful warmth
Dancing midst the beautiful nature around.

But, Oh my dear!
I cannot watch in silence
A poverty ridden child or a destined orphan.

DISPIRITED

A new theme creeps
But unfortunate….
There's no pen, no paper
Where to scribble it?

Memory cannot treasure
Such sudden gush of musings
In vain, it may try yet
But helpless, it withdraws, yes.

Like the silence after storm
Like the calmness after sunset
Thoughts reduce to rubble
Like particles withdrawn ashore

Yes, a new theme creeps
But memory fails to hold sway
Dispirited, it slowly fades away
Into the perpetual past, helpless!

THE YEARNING

Before the first rays
From the eastern horizon
Dawn upon you …..
You greet me as usual
To brighten my drowsy eyes.

The beautiful colors
A real feast to eyes,
Your delightful fragrance
Overwhelmed, marches past
Stirring a new spirit in heart.

Alas! But, I feel dejected
For you are bound to wither
With the fall of dusk….
Destined, you have no tomorrow
So also any sorrow, perhaps!

How many flowers inspire me
Through my bed-room window
Dawn after dawn reappears,
Years keep piling behind.

The theory and theme of life
Still aim to know the ultimate
What could be the disparity
Betwixt the theory and theme
I fail to assess …
Still aspiring to know more.

PROMISES

New initiatives for world peace
At last should see the light here,
Showering petals of happiness
They should spread joy and brightness
Yes, a streak of new peace vision
Should enlighten every vision and tenor.

Let's pray God for universal peace
Let's seek God to shower his grace
Love can succeed any great enemy
Trust can spread joy, without a penny
Yes, New peace initiatives
It's ripe time, should wipe many a fear.

Each morrow should become a milestone
Paving way to build a prosperous home
Yes, let's eliminate the violent tendencies
Let's eradicate mis-apprehensions and mistrust
Yes, a new resolve should unite us
With a resolve for peace and a promise for bliss.

GAIN WISDOM

Have you noticed my filthy clothes
I have an inclination, an imagination
To be as rich and afresh as nature, but
My inner life strikes an emotive chord
How I had turned old, shadowed by age.

Have you noticed my diluting thoughts
I have a mission, a far fetching vision
To serve humanity till my energy permits
But, bone-sucked, neglected and alone
Fate had struck me, shadowing my aims.

When the spirit was high, the aim was aloof
Now, when the aim is high, the spirit is aloof
The passing time has piled in more strafe
Just to strangle myself, midst grappling grief.

Remember! Time and tide wait for none
We have to make hay while the sun shines
Past is past, look at the looming tomorrow
Gain some wisdom, to bask under a new morrow.

AGITATE MEMORIES

How can I consider how the light is spent
When in the past, in this dark world and wild
I failed to enlighten own wisdom in right spirit,
Engulfed with selfish thoughts and deeds.

Now, when I try to free out from that tide
Heart-broken and ashamed, I feel out at sea,
So many years had I drained on the futile side
Ignorant of human sufferings and orphan pleas.

Its too late perhaps, but better late than never
Some humanitarian service should I render
Lest, the darkness shall surround me forever
Leaving a permanent void in life, without temper.

Thoughts become young with renewed spirits,
But, tears trickle down my fast ageing cheeks
Agitate memories try to bask under new sparks
With the sole aim to over run the past life freaks.

THE ULTIMATE FEAR

The recurring memories
Like clouds of emotion
Surge out, all of a sudden
From the volcano of musings.

The mourning dreams
Assemble in the irises of eyes,
Desires flirt in search of joys
Foreseeing my pathetic fate.

The eclipsed charming world
The love-filled ecstatic waves
Embalm the bleeding wounds,
It's too late to undo the damage.

Where do the musings re-appear?
Why do they strike in repetition?
Memories resume and boil like lava
As if to stoke the ultimate storm.

THE INNER LIGHT

The light of peace
Into my mind peeps
You too possess the light
Dear, cannot you explore it?

There's wisdom in the caged thoughts
There's wisdom in the wrapped up mind
Unlock the never-ending desires
Unfurl and ignite the sparks of fire.

The fire is light, of course
It can lit the paths of future course
Let's attain the freedom to explore
Dreams can become real, my dear.

Refresh and re-look into the past
Gain something from the lost gist
Yes, the gist of peace is peeled alarmingly
It bleeds, yes it bleeds on incessantly.

Humanity, at the brink of losing its instinct
Needs a recuperating touch from all sects
Let the inner light glow, let not it fade away
Let's struggle to uplift human values everyday.

THE SNOW

The tepid rays of the winter Sun
Strike the snowy mountain peaks,
The silver-glittery reflections
Implant a delightful, memorable view.

The transformation
The horizon
The vision ….
Though raptures everyone
Give a momentary relief
From worry and grief,
Can it but eventually influence
The human instinct of compassion.

Here and there, in ignored reality
Bogged down in deep penury
Shaken by violence and uncertainty
People writhe with pain and hunger.
But can someone provide real succor
To uplift their sagging morale of survival,
Midst the struggle for a morsel of food
Giving a new hope and destination.

Transform! Oh human, transform
Like the snow, which slowly melts
Like the beams, which gently soothe
Let the heart slowly melt and gently reach
The garden of love longing flowers
Where, humane instinct can stoke our wisdom.

HUMAN INSTINCT

The buzy streets of metro cities
Hold beautiful, apart from ugly sights
Some desperate and desolate souls
Strike our hearts, if looked through.

Ignorantly the passerby pass
A bit of human instinct, I feel
Cannot someone offer to spare
To uplift human moral for a real cause.

A good samaritan perhaps
Hold an orphaned child on her lap
His bone-sucked face, brights up
His deep sunk eyes, lift up
But, his weak, malnourished body
Struggle to hold the last atom of life.

Like a stray dog, banished
A pathetic child midst millions of people,
Writhingly breathe his last ….
Followed by similar recurrence.

The city pathways are beautiful
Of course, the interiors are awful
Hearts would sink, tears would gush out
Pour out your heart into that sphere, please!

A POEM FOR THE LIFE

I have seen
Much life of this world
Afraid …..
I question, am I blind?
Of course …
You too stand a mute spectator
Ignorant of the happenings around.

The invaluable human lives
The beautiful natural resources
The scintillating and rotund moon
The smooth flowing silent rivers
How peaceful they look!
How pretty they resemble!

The drizzle of the rainy season
The song of the Koel during spring
The evening wind blow during summer
The shining dew at the dawn of winter,
I have been a witness to these delights
Sparing year after year with hesitation.

'cause on the other side of this delight
I find violent and unimaginable plight
An undernourished child, a starving mother
A devoid life, midst poverty and fears
Slowly drift through an era of illusions, yes
Seasons change, but not the human values
Who's going to infuse the lacking instinct.

MIDST THE SILENCE

Silently I watch
Moment after moment
Slip away into eternity.

Silently I feel
The invisible layers of wind
Blow past into perpetuity.

Silently I glimpse
Tide after tide in the sea
Get gulped by another tide.

Silently I glance
The delightful buds
Blossom by the passing of night.

And silently I aspire
To fly like a home-coming bird
Across the horizon of setting Sun

Yes, silently I dream
To experience the bountiful warmth
Of the beautiful nature around us.

But …. Oh my dear!
I cannot watch in silence
A starving child or a war-torn place.

ENLIGHTENMENT

Seek the light of God
To share the tenderness of love
Seek the light of love
To share the feelings of faith
Seek the light of faith
To share the compassion of peace
Seek the light of Peace
To share the ultimate of passion
Seek the path of passion
To discover a source for salvation.

Let human instinct within, be awakened
Weeding out the obstacles of wisdom ….
A supreme glow will fill thy heart
Where the doors of wisdom lay wide open,
…. while a peace-filled phase invokes you.

Between the fleeing stint of life and death
Let the bondage of humanity stay eternal
Yes, seek thy God, Love, Faith and Peace
The essence of wisdom will enlighten forever.

THE AMALGAMATION

The showers are soon to welcome
Waiting for some specific moments to come
The flowers of joy shall blossom very soon
The clouds shall envelope the Sun during noon.

Yes, the breeze shall carry the fragrance
Which would flow out of the flowery essence,
Musings afresh would gush out with glee
Like a honeybee, as if midst the lush trees.

Carried away by waves of thoughtful stupor
The pen wields at will on the plain paper
Lines flow in torrents, without any respite
Aspiring to compose a new poem, right!

A feast of refined poetry is bound to unfurl
Pray! Each moment should hold standstill
But, PEACE should be the theme and option
Which should adorn such rare amalgamation.

IN QUEST OF AMITY

Build the bond of love and friendship
Which shall bring us closer and closer
Close enough to a lasting relationship
Which shall bind us together, ever and forever.

Let us strive to enjoy a new dawn of peace
To add a new feather to its heart-warming chorus
Faith and amity can make this a beautiful place,
A place to bask under the warm love-filled rays.

The enormous loss of human lives each day
With shades of revengeful slaughter creeping on,
Won't the pathetic state of innocents hold sway
To render love and care to the tormented human.

We all know, hatred to co-exist curtails peace
Is it not the root cause for the prevailing evils?
Why can't we exhibit our wit, patience and tolerance
To sort out surfacing differences and other frictions.

Yes, let's strive to give a chance for PEACE….
Our inner strength and dedication to attain it
Fails to get fulfilled, unless others support us
Yes, let's join hands atleast now, to achieve it.

OH GOD! LET ME

Pray you, Oh Dear God
Bless me with the spirit of worship
Bless me with the power of wisdom
Mould me to render humanitarian service
But don't make me a selfish zealot.

Though am grown up
Oh Lord! With trust in you I pray
Don't make merry of my future
Instead respond as if I am your son.

I aspire to learn more and be helpful
But if you disown, I may waste my life
Shower and impart love and faith
To enable me to shine and excel
In every field, at every mile
With blessings to render humane service.

Yes, I shall be a great person
Willing to make triumphant beginnings
This life is indebted to you
Let me enable to share it with love.

THE PURSUIT

I feel agitate without any right cause to know
But perhaps its your love, hid long long ago
Yes, those pleasant memories I can never forego
Though am quite old and fading out, I know.

Though am alone, I had many a companion
With the beautiful nature around to fascinate
The poetic musings often stir around and oscillate
Scribbling one after the other solitary tune thereon.

The stirring babble of flocks of homecoming birds
The striking rays of early dawn through the mountains
The spiraling flow of streams surrounding the terrain
What a scenic beauty with colourful flowers and buds.

But still to no avail, the scenic, eye-feasting beauty
Still rocks my heart for you at this bewitching hour
These moments drag me into an eternal trauma
Outwitting the past delights, into the dark future.

IF NOT ......

The monsoon showers are soon to welcome
Waiting for some lovelorn moments to come
The flowers of joy shall blossom very soon
The clouds shall envelope the sun during noon.

The breeze shall carry the intoxicant fragrance
Which would gush out of the flowery essence,
Like a honeybee encircling midst the lush trees
Musings afresh would stream out with glee.

Carried away by waves of thoughtful stupor
The pen wields at will on the plain paper
Lines flow in torrents without any respite
Aspiring to compose poems anew with delight!

In memory of death-defying love, I hauntingly hurl
A feast of romantic poetry is bound to unravel
Lo! She has painted my life and it's destination
If not, I cannot be a poet wielding the romantic pen.

A SANCTORUM OF PEACE

Lo! The so called protectors of peace
Why not the wars could be averted
Lo! The devastators of peace
What's the sin of the innocents feared dead.

Not only are you pounding the enemy
But harming the own mother earth as well
Silently she's writhing with agony
Aren't we duty bound to safeguard it, tell?

Here and there, under the war-torn rubble
Accursed as if, innocents ripped to death
Mourners gather to pay their last tributes
Perhaps to pay a tearful homage to 'faith'.

The tears that trickle down like a pool of blood
The blood that flows like a stream of river
Aggravate the earth's deep inflicted wounds ….
Is our next generation cursed to bear the nightmare.

Thoughts likewise, on to the war front gallop
I feel the trauma, the suffering and the pain
Cannot our concealed wisdom move forward a step
To arouse the passion for peace, hid in every human.

Why can't we be a part in restoring "peace" forever
To make our planet earth "A SANCTORUM OF PEACE'.

BETWIXT DELIGHTS

In a flash, buildings shook
Rocked by a violent impact
A bomb dropped
With revengeful ferocity.
A nerve shocking view
Everything reduced to ash
A heart-rending scene
That can never erase from eyes.
Scores of innocents killed
Many at the doorstep of death
Small children to teen-aged boys
All lay shocked by the havoc
Almost dead, yet with an iota of life
Entire families wiped out
In a single devastating stroke
Whom to blame, whom to curse?

Perhaps the nation may be re-built
The pride of ravaged cities be restored
But alas!
Who can bring back a lost life?
Who can restore the limbs of the disabled?
Who can pour life to a lost mother?
Who can provide the priceless parental care?
Cursed are the sufferers
Midst the delights of the triumph
Who would love them
If their own motherland lay bleeding.

LET US SAY.....

Say NO - to the partisan approach and forcible invasions
Say NO - to the prejudiced and unwarranted incursions
Say NO - to the cross border terrorism and suicidal attacks
Say NO - to the devastating and life-crippling bombings
Say NO - to the inhuman and barbaric killings
Say NO - to the violent acts of global terrorism
Say NO - to the conflicts of aggression for supremacy
Say NO - to the future hostilities to avert global catastrophe
Say NO - to the environmental disasters and human suffering

Yes, where are we heading to ....
Oh dear humans, let us stay united and pledge to say ......

Yes ... for imparting lessons of Peace and non-violence
Yes ... for curbing the deep-rooted hatred
Yes .... for curtailing the deep feelings of vengeance
Yes .... for quelling the threat of ecological imbalances
Yes .... for seeking restrain from sectarian and religious aggression
Yes .... for restraining the desires of attaining superiority
Yes .... for abridging the selfish deeds of despotism (dictatorship)
Yes .... for uplifting human values and sheltering the needy
YES ... FOR RESTORING PEACE AND AMITY IN THE WORLD.

THE DISORDER

Ferocity, the character of war
When raise its revengeful hood
No doubt, instills shock and fear
Prompting a grave fear psyche

Hatred and grudge, given a chance
Vie to quench their eternal thirst
Leaving scars of un-imaginable havoc,
Shocking humanity with a catastrophic jolt.

Helpless, as mute spectators we stand
To the relentless volatile events that recur
'cause we fail to co-exist in harmony
There's no remedy to avert the global horror.

In the garb of sacred war, it's another furore
The petals of peace are torn and thrown
A hapless child gasps with traumatic fear
While others mourn their near and dear kin

Lo! where are we heading to, haunts me often.
Encircled by ecological wreck and crying orphans.

A SOURCE FOR REFUGE

Fleeting time, fleeting time
Sets its tune with its fleeing rhyme
Time and tide, yes, wait for none
Promised, they keep their eternal run.

A moment passed can never return
Another impending moment wait its turn
Promised, the day and night occur and recur
Never looking back in their fleeing stupor.

With promises to keep, born as mortals
We have to abide by them till the final ritual
Being guests in the Lord's unbound shelter
Let us not be slaves to the external glitters.

Having ravaged our own nests with passions
Past has taught us many far-sighted lessons
With grudge and deceit, many of us got ruined
With short-lived selfishness, ignominy was gained.

We are duty bound to co-exist in peace
We are duty bound to protect the values of peace
But we have no regard to either of them
Vying always to fight for supremacy and fame.

Trust has been lost, became a dream dear
Poor became poorer, rich became wealthier
Rocked by mass killings, violence and strife
No succor to the needy and no refuge for life.

Yes, at this hour of turmoil and humiliation
Why not we seek refuge at the Lord's bastion.

TRAUMA AND FURORE

Ferocity, the character of violence and war
When raise its vengeful and venomous hood
No doubt, mistrust and fright get implanted
Prompting a grave fear psyche in everyone.

Hatred and grudge, if given a chance
Vie to quench their thirst, once and for all
Leaving scars of un-imaginable havoc,
Shocking humanity with a catastrophic jolt.

Helpless, as mute spectators we stand
To the relentless and volatile events that recur
Because we fail to co-exist as co-humans
How can there be a remedy for the horror?

In the garb of sacred war, it's another furore
The petals of peace are torn and thrown
A hapless child gasps with traumatic fear
While others mourn their near and dear kin

Lo! where are we heading to, haunts me often.
Encircled by ecological wreck and crying orphans.

THE CONFESSION

When the dreams of childhood
Were about to flourish forthwith
You turned them into a nightmare
To shatter my dreams, with vengeance.

When the charms of youth
Were about to delight for a while
You scratched me without mercy
Leaving a perpetual vacuum.

When the buds of childish love
Were about to blossom forthwith
You plucked them in a fit of rage
To plunge me into an emotive vortex.

When I was set to sail-off
For a brief joy ride in the life's boat
You stroked it to get capsized
Midst the tempest of uncertainty.

Without a spark of hope
Without a trace of luck
Lo destiny! Why do you hunt me
Without any respite and mercy.

If life itself is a deceit
As destiny, if you justify your role;
I salute you for the devotion
Tired and vexed, I concede my defeat.

FREAK INVASIONS

Our beautiful love would unfurl tonight
Paving way for a new bondage to sprout
The merry moments grace with delight
To celebrate the event after a long long wait.

But, the pitiable sight of the wilting flowers
The sprouting plight of buds, nipped forever,
The emotionally doused heart of jilted lovers
All in all, pounce to torture me at this hour.

Darkness sneak through the delightful clouds
Thoughts overthrow me onto woe-filled moods
With ravaging memories at this hour of delight
I struggle to encounter the unexpectant torment.

The moon and stars adorn the gorgeous sky
The beautiful nature, delights every eye
The lurking dawn of tomorrow, far behind treetops
Pelf or passion, yes cannot counter this joys scope

Yet I fear, am I unfortunate and an accursed lot
To get carried away by such invading thoughts
Or is it a lesson for life, to know and to get taught
Giving ample scope for an insight on future delights

IN AWAIT OF A NEW DAWN

Casting so little of light on our lives
Keeping most of us under a dark spell
Lord! Is it the way you opt to punish us
Keeping peace and prosperity at stake
Hampering the little wisdom we possess.

Oh divine and miraculous God …
Are we the accursed generations?
Or mere fabricated tools of your game
Displacing everything at will and wish
You jolt the mankind with wars, calamities.

Half-way through, half-way to explore still
Is there no way out to end human miseries
The heart-rending starvation deaths
The aftermath of war-related devastations,
We still feel trailing an unknown destination.

Can the starving lot, hope for some relief
Can the war ravaged, hope for some peace
Can the drought hit be appeased with rains
Can the peace efforts yield desired results
If by Gods grace the outcome is positive
No doubt! A new dawn is bound to usher
Salvaging the lost faith with a lasting trust.

Yes, throwing some more light on our lives
Oh God! Keep us spellbound with your miracles
This is the way you ought to uplift our spirits
Blessing humanity with a new dawn of peace, yes
With enlightened insight, we all shall taste success.

EVASIVE INSTINCT

Across the slums, thoughts strike
Whenever an insight I provoke
The very thought of downtrodden
Bulldoze my thoughts quite often.
The darkness which rule their hearts
Devoid of even a spark of light
Atleast a spark of mercy can't it possess.
A naked child's weeping crawl
Through the skeletons of hunger
Provoke to curse the so-called fate
Apart from blaming the human instinct too.

Cuddled, a lifeless mother
On the verge of her last breath
A caring father, almost exhaustive
Caught in the vortex of penury
Either a rudder or a log to rescue,
Every frantic effort seems elusive.
Grief is all, which is left to greet them
Hunger is the sole companion
To haunt, torment and frustrate.
Between these recurring hassles
How can an instinct exist for survival?

HARMONIOUS PATH

Violence is not an answer to violence
It's an immature action of intolerance
Not that we expose the potion of vengeance
But patience and love to break the imbalance.

Appeasement is not cowardice, but mental maturity
That shall prove right, when dust settles slowly
Try to reckon, where the fault dwells within you
Let the tendency sow in others too, sharing love.

Pave way for the peace process with truth and trust
Inspire others to march through, without any haste
Wean away the paths for supremacy through violence
Lead others to the harmonious path with non-violence.

Through "Harmonious Path" one can definitely pass
When self-confidence advances in the right process.

THE BARREN SCAPES
OF SOLITUDE

at once, in a sudden gush
A stormy cloud envelop my life
It drifts through heart of hearts
Stirring a new phase of painful sort.

Though duty bound and destined,
The storm perhaps feel by heart
To sympathize my trickling tears.
Possessing the imposing power
To ignite a perpetual havoc
Breaking my dreams to fragments,
It can even cool-off with a welcome
By aspiring to embrace me
With an everlasting happiness,
No doubt, ever fancied.

My already deserted life
Though readied for confrontation
A streak of hope still sneaks
To perceive a garden of roses
Before being completely routed
In the barren scapes of solitude.

HOW CAN YOU .....

Entangled in between
Absurd poverty and hunger;
In the day-to-day life,
Eyes confront mercy-filled tears.

The hour after hour pounce
Of the dreadful hunger
Spreading its fatal tentacles
Deep into poverty-ridden slums;
Still tending for a hungry dance
In search of another victim;
Certainly a heart stirring scene
Bound to stay deep, eternally.

In this uncertain phase
Life cannot be a garden of roses
And, when thorns are prone to prick
Life cannot anticipate for peace.
Plundering poverty to bleed yet
With renewed grudge for supremacy,
Humanity unfolds its true colors.
Then, how can you seek
And yes, how can you question
The sanctity of peace and prosperity.

THE MARCHING TIME

You did not turn-up,
The marching time however drew on
I felt a pain of new sort
Having lost the hope's spark.
In disbelief and dejection
The circumstances I couldn't overcome
Dumbstruck by the sudden outcome.

The colourful and cozy dreams
Woven on the bliss of love charms
Lay shattered across the golden arch
At the garden of roses, on their march,
Only to wriggle out of the traumatic path
In search of an answer to the broken faith.

With lost hopes and incompatible strife
Carried away midst the ocean of grief,
With a broken heart and broken dreams
I know, against this tide I cannot swim
Without any hope to salvage my bleak future
That's set to bequeath an indelible scar.

While the delicate petals of trust lay strewn
With the broken and bewildered aspirations,
So are the depths of my trust, oh my dear
Failing to counter the upsurge of unknown fear.
Yes, *the marching time* has already over-run
Leaving a perpetual vacuum, forever drawn.

CANONIZATION

The dreaded missile …
Tores apart the silent skies;
Sow the seeds of destruction
Endangering life on earth.
Yet it carves a name of its own
Giving fame to nations and scientists
In unveiling a new conventional fear
Solely aimed at devastating something.

Engagement of enormous toil and finance
For its invention and (mis) utilisation
Is bound to destroy all welfare objectives
Thus weakening the growth of economy,
Ultimately burdening the common man
With the pinch of hardship and uncertainty.

The quest to be superior in warfare,
To emboss "triumph" over the weak
To sow the seeds of destruction
Of course, is a show put-up for superiority.
No doubt….
On one hand
We boast of superior technology
While on the other side of the same,
Leave imprints of destruction
Defacing the basic element and morale
Of both the peace and prosperity.

THE PARTING

Dear, under the night's decesive eyes
The time has cursed us to get apart,
Dawn would soon befall from eastern skies
Breaking our longings and feelings apart.

But, neither do I have the yearning
Nor do I possess any destined leaning
Dejected, I seek the night's blessing
To behold like a flower, though wilting.

The flower posses a short span of life
Likewise, the dark clouds that drifts
The rain showers, to please the host
The aroma flows to intoxicate the grief.

The skies would glitter when it dawns
The birds would fly-off with joy unbound
Though my love-lorn dreams lay cursed
Close to heart, the doomed song draws.

I know, I must obey the gallows of fate
Though parting, the trauma still haunts
My tryst with destiny, I should salute
'cause the dawn lurks in haste to sneak out.

AT WHOSE BEHEST

Yes, I stood in a traumatic silence
To see an orphan struggle...
Struggle to overcome life's hassles
For a fistful of food
For a moment of parental warmth.

I had seen the flowers wither in haste
Fearing a storm that would ravage soon.
Yes, what's the fate of the buds
Dreaming to see the light of tomorrow,
If their own origin would uproot today.

I had seen the thunder of clouds
Move menacingly to overrun the mid-day
Yes, they are destined to hobnob with ruin
Amongst the fields, amongst the poor slums
In a bid to further deprive the hope-starved.

What if, if love prevails amongst all
The poor would be happy, also their hopes
The orphans get clasped with parental warmth
The cozy flowers will aspire to adorn the Lord
At whose behest only, it's all-possible, Oh Lord!

NIGHTMARE

Torn is the sky between the day and night
The hours of impatience roll too slowly
My love bears no luck, except a lonely fright
Nowhere delights resemble, just stumble

Though, like a creeper
Around the 'LOVE' stem I creep
No sign could I glimpse as yet
To reach the nectar, much sought after.

The stars do not twinkle, though its midnight
Hid behind dark clouds, without any delight
Hours painfully lapse in quest of something
The dawn would soon befall, Lo! It's lurking.

When once and for all the dreams surged,
Later when destiny with vengeance emerged
Years did lapse, but without any beatitude
Scuttling every dream without any gratitude.

What if the sea of love overflows the shore
When doomed aspirations are hurtled ashore
Though the vows swim against the currents
Down the solitude, I face irresistible torments.

My dear, Yes, without you oh my dear!
The pangs I experience, resemble a nightmare.

THE BREACH

A breach of love, the trauma of a broken heart
Ache gets implanted, cannot be plucked again;
In the aftermath of betrayal, heart kneels to fate
Stroking wound after wound, bleeding with pain.

Neither the day quickly sets, nor the night
The wilting flowers prostrate in deep dejection
No dream to dream for a sparkling delight
No hope to rejoice or glimpse a brief fruition.

Yes, the stars twinkle and the moon glows
The sun relapses from the horizon as usual
But for love's quest, sacrificial heart bows
Though days and years lapse midst the travails.

Accursed is the heart, stormed by jilted love
The citadel of fortune bids to declare homage
Thorns do prick where attraction prevails, how?
Yes, to endure it, we ought to face some ravage.

Lo! The walls of heart shall breach and break
When the deluge of love uncovers its fury
Betwixt devil and deep sea, life dangles at stake
Ashore can it swim or survive the breach of fury.

A PROMISE FOREVER

When the wind favored me against all the odds
I sought refuge at Lord to surpass future hassles
When again the storms tried to recur; I faced
Despite all, I could at last reach the love castle.

Like a blossoming flower, its afresh and beautiful
The fragrance intoxicate me in a fit of stupor
The moments should not eclipse, I pray heartful
To boost memories for an everlasting hangover.

Storms often occur and recur, they are fierce too
In a routine, the onset of seasons too recur
But the sole season embedded in heart, is love
Which can confront any storm, without a any fear.

Perhaps the goddess of love favours everything
Her blessings can stem any ominous storms
What more should I seek at this hour of longing
Except bestowing heartfelt thanks, full of warmth.

Let during the day or night, either joy or sorrow
Heart shall engulf with love, crave for each other
This is *a promise forever*, not today, not tomorrow
Yes, proudly I acclaim, we are made for each other.

BREAK-EVEN POINT

To break the trust
To bridge the trust
Which one is easier
Unhesitantly the first.

To gain love
To break love
Easier than the said one
Is no doubt, gaining love.

To bestow life is great
To take life is deceit
The gifted life of human
Yes, is the Lord's aspiration.

Plant a seed to see it sprout
Growth looks beautiful, no doubt
Flowers will spread fragrance
Fragrance in turn, love & romance.

The cry of an orphan dear
The hunger of a roadside beggar
Bereft of mercy, we avoid, yes
O! Service to humanity! My God!
Reckon, is service rendered to God
Let our inner-self succeed
Wherein our wit dwells unbound.

Yes, no bud would desire
To be nipped in the bud itself
No flower would aspire
To be plucked before the sun rise
Yet, the omnipresent miracle prevails
Playing the tunes at God's will
Where lurks the break-even point.

THE THOUGHT OF TOMORROW

the gentle breeze swings in the nature's lap
With the golden moon-lit night's brilliance
The swinging echo of its euphoric spell traps
Set afree as if, in the beautiful horizon for a dance.

The nocturnal delight is a heart-warming feast
Seeing naughty stars play behind the snowy clouds
The tiny buds into the charming flowers promote
And the amusing colours resemble a rainbow flood.

But somewhere, someone at a dark street corner
On a footpath shivers, a half-naked poor beggar
Betwixt unimaginative death, a hellish life staggers
Tonight, the dark blanket may wrap him forever.

The thought of tomorrow, the dawn of tomorrow
Engulf the delight with a surging spell of sorrow
Thoughts may pause but not the time, it runs fast
Soon, the phase will disappear into the invisible past.

CHARMING NIGHT

Look at the glowing sky, the twinkling stars
Fascinating and soul stirring is the nature.

Yes, the breeze with a gentle love song flows
The moonlight with a golden brilliancy glows
The delicate tree tops swing in an euphoric glee
Ablaze is the beautiful horizon with stars set afree.

The nocturnal blend is indeed memorable
How nice if the passing time remain standstill
Peace will reign the scales of every thought
The fortress of love will submerse in delight.

Lucky are the flowers which during nights bloom
Lucky are the buds which for a tomorrow dream
Lucky are the clouds adorning the sky every night
Lucky are those who cherish the adorable sight.

The thought of tomorrow, the dawn of tomorrow
Engulf the very delight with a tide of sorrow
Time do not pause, we may stop, but not the time
The phase will disappear paving way for other rhyme.

REFUGE

A prisoner of thoughts is any poet's heart
Where any thought can easily stir the poet,
Any thought can easily stroke the poet,
Any eventuality can easily entice the poet.

The consecrate affiliation with poetic surge
Yet the isolation midst the urban populace,
Afloat still in the vortex of theme is a new one
Unless another concept creeps, no doubt it dwells.

Autumn leaves flutter with the morning gales
Dew drops glitter under the reflective sunrays
The golden horizon unfold its delights, yes
Soft and cool, a dream dawns in thoughts castle.

Anticipated, a surge of musings freak out
Being a poet, I feel imprisoned in own fort
May be yet another theme sneaks to sow a seed
Before the present tendency is set to retreat.

The urban phenomenon curbs my aspirations
My quest for beautiful nature casts an aspersion
Though am midst all comforts and riches
The confronting thoughts seek nature's refuge.

URBAN PSYCHE

Silently I watch
Moment after moment
Slowly slip into eternity.

Silently I feel
The invisible layers of wind
Blow past into perpetuity.

Silently I glimpse
Tide after tide in the sea
Get swallowed by another tide.

Silently I glance
The delightful buds
Blossom by the passing of night.

And silently I aspire
To fly like a home-coming bird
Across the golden horizon of setting Sun

Yes, silently I dream
To experience the bountiful warmth
Dancing midst the beautiful nature around.

But, Oh my dear!
I cannot watch in silence
A poor orphan discarded by urban psyche.

DRIVING THE PAINS OUT

Dreams emerge out in endless continuity
Where I encounter a deep longing for joys
Caught betwixt surroundings of nature's bounty
Dreams illumine the horizon of thought's skies.

The pretty butterflies, their eye-feasting colours
The beautiful birds, their high flying feats
The beautiful snow-covered mountains afar
The slow swirling stream at the mountain feet.

In my teens, when I was energetic and young
I never had a tendency to watch this beauty
Selfish, I spent life in the city suburban sting
Mindful of life's lasting association with duty.

When whatever seems possessed in life seem lost
And when solitude overpowered every thought
Engulfed and aroused, I stood by nature's delight
Lost in pensive dreams, driving all other pains out.

WHEN SHALL WE AWAKEN

At midnight, under the moonlight
I stand beneath, with a drowsy delight.

The reflection, re-reflects through stars,
The high tides crash out of the seashore
The gales carry their joy-filled messages
The moon steps down the mountain ridge

The blooming buds and the pretty flowers
Long to douse in this moonlit shower
This beautiful night is their first and last
Tomorrow's dusk fall may curse them to wilt.

A night-loving bird sings a glee-filled song,
Carried away by the wind currents, so strong
The voice vibrates in tune with the sea tides
Perhaps to inspire the sprouting flowers pride.

Yet, behind the core of the mundane splendor
The little hearts of beautiful birds and flowers
Beat with a wail of fear about the uncertain future
Caught midst the man-made ecological disasters.

When shall we awaken from the heedless slumber
Though often nature hints us the imminent dangers.

GIVE "PEACE"
ANOTHER CHANCE

the fires of death and hatred, dance
Re-emerging with more vengeance
For some, death is a form of martyrdom
Self-imposed, in the name of religious idiom.

But, the soiled inner-self should change
The impulse of fanaticism should change
Given another chance, "Peace" shall stay
The world can see a change within a day.

With backing by the showers of trust
The seeds of love shall slowly sprout
The petals of faith shall fling with glee
In prosperity, every nation shall we see.

The roots of evil…. poverty and starvation
The hassles of development…. aggression
When both are resisted by self-motivation
The earth shall become an abode of heaven.

Instead of destruction, we witness growth
Instead of hatred, we feel love and warmth
The clouds of passion shall spring a new trust
The winds of change shall blow every mistrust.

Yes, even if the fires of death and hatred, dance
Yes, let's seek to give "Peace" another chance.

MERCY

The showers may disappear soon
Crops may flourish like a boon
Yet poverty unfolds in every sphere
Without vent, throughout the year
The thirst of death doesn't end here
Till an alternate is shown the door.

Hunted by death, trampled by hunger
Poverty knocks the tolerance of poor
Where do the strings of MERCY dwell?
The answer is evasive as well.
Cursed by fate, accursed by destiny
Their poor plight is set to lose the battle
Yet, can the sole string of mercy …..
Show mercy at the doorway of fading hopes.

WHEN REALISM DAWNS

Disregarded all through the years
My heart, my hearth and home
For you, I have a deep longing
To reach the unending quest, my dear!

Hours and days have been devoured
Ruthless, the oasis of joy was squeezed
Colourful dreams have been trampled
The very thought of hope, seem lynched.

All of a sudden, from out of the dark
When the lost hope emerge like a spark;
Drifting moments of palpable impatience
Stand dazed in unknown trance, at once.

A streak of radiance, defuse my isolation
A streak of joy ignite my preoccupied vision
The unending wait, presumed immeasurable
No doubt, shall now repeal all the hassles.

The suffering spent all through the years
When bids adieu at this fag end of misery,
No doubt, fate holds an iota of mercy too
And the one I yearn, certainly will brace me.

IN THE NIGHT PUB

There …… yes ….
For the rich intoxicated thugs
Money is a rotten thing
Thrown on semi-naked bodies.

Sparsely dressed bevy of beauties
With vivacious curved bodies
Swing to the loud musical notes
Staking their chaste for a loot
To douse the carnal pleasures
On a thick layers of currency.

The notes of platonic love
Stir the drowsy love-lorn hearts
Lashed by the emotive tides
They arouse the jilted hearts.
Inflamed…. the jilted hearts
Search r a shelter to seek solace
But, shocked beyond belief
Discover the impure garb of love.

The ever-evasive money
The sacrificial instinct of love
Both sacred and the scarcest
So cheap are they displayed here
To simply fit the wallet of the rich
To dance to the rich tunes, at will.

TORN APART

Heart aches, shattered dreams peep through pains
Though drunk, intoxication fails to confiscate me
The engulfing emotion, pricks like sharp thorns
Stirring an unending trauma. Gasping, will it sink me.

Does every dark cloud possess a silver lining?
Can a bright phase end on a dismal dark note
How cruel is the fate to clip your budding wings
No words do I find to scatter an emotive quote.

The stars have been twinkling for ages
The oceans have been swirling for ages
Their unquenched thirst still flows with a rage
While a dumb life fade away into past's mirage.

Though withstood the cold wave of the winter
You lay exposed to the hottest summer noon
The moon-lit night still drags me close, dear!
Without your presence, it can knock me down.

But, if fate plays the game of love with destiny
Befooled, hearts torn apart we seek deaths shelter
Now….of what use are these riches and money
Soon should I be laid down deep the earth's layers.

The nightingale I adore is ravaged by doom, yes
The starry nights and lyrical gales carry no bliss.

MIDST ILLUSIONS

Midst the stars of blinking thoughts
My mind glows like a full moon
The cloud is a paper, plain and white
Jotting few lines now, indeed is a boon.

I know the thunder of drifting clouds
I know the tenderness of a hazy rainbow
But the pathetic state of the dry clouds
Strike some dissent in thoughts borough.

Conveying to mind the earthly miseries
Joy experiences nothing in solitude
Encircled by uncertainty, it too suffers
Midst the silent valley of fading fortitude.

Imagine the amusement of nature
Two pigeons play side by side and flirt
Their joy is joy, their world is theirs
Indoor, a world of new sort is painted.

An entire world fits in the lake of illusion
Like a pebble of solitude if it is thrown
Ripples are drawn to the shore in confusion
Where joys of isolation will ultimately drown.

LET'S ASPIRE TO ......

Often the fires of death and hatred, dance
Re-emerging with more vengeful vigor
For some, death is a form of martyrdom
Self-imposed in the kingdom of fanaticism.

When the soiled inner-self seeks a change
The impulse of fanaticism also changes
Given another chance, "Peace" shall stay
The world should foresee this change, I pray.

With the showering patronage of trust
The seeds of love slowly shall sprout
The petals of faith shall unfurl with fruition
Prosperity shall dawn on every nation.

The roots of evil…. poverty and starvation
The hassles of development…. aggression
When both are resisted by self-motivation
Mother Earth shall become an abode of heaven.

Instead of destruction, we witness growth
Bereft of hatred, we sense the love's warmth
The clouds of passion shall spring a new trust
The winds of change shall blow every mistrust.

Yes, even if the fires of death and hatred, dance
Yes, let's aspire to give "Peace" another chance.

A DREAM REAL

Ferocity, the face of war
When with vengeance it roars
Death would dance at every yard
Humanity weeps at the graveyard.

Peace seems uprooted
Rejected, it emotively bleeds
Somewhere, someone tries to retrieve
With few takers, it opts to retire.

The annals of history
Cannot forgive us later
Why not we act a bit flexible
To make PEACE, a dream real.

THE LIGHT OF WISDOM

The desire to possess riches
The inkling to enjoy luxuries,
Perturbed with such greedy desires
O human, why you seek such breach.

Have you not ignored the poor
Have the seeds of hatred sowed not
Yet with unrelenting discontent
You are knocking the sinner's door.

The inner light of wisdom
Is enveloped by the selfish face
Why not you seek some solace
To be a part of a cherished dream.

THE BARRIERS

Though made out of clay
You make the children play
The beauty you possess
TOYS! Indeed is enormous.

Implanted by tender kisses
And warm hugs
You impart life's lessons
Through intimate silence.

Trust is life, love is life
Tryst with destiny is also life
No scope for worries
If understood the life's barriers.

NO WHERE TO ESCAPE

Times …. good and bad
Moments quick and slow
Move on before they fade
While the flowers of life glow.

Memories fade into the past
The fountain of fleeting age
Gallops for a transitory respite
Yes, life cannot escape this cage.

With no place to escape
And nowhere to escape,
Betwixt the life's landscape
Lead the life on tomorrow's hope.

TOMORROW SEEMS ......

The fleeting time fascinates
Leaving us far behind, at times
Seasons are destined to come
Fading into eternity within no time.

Joys and sorrows frequent at times
Flowers of peace get rattled by storms
Lackluster are some surging moments
Instigative too are a few life's moments.

A shout for peace at a war-torn corner
A scream for a fist of food at another
The shadow of death dance at both ends
Feasting on innocents who are dead.

The war for peace is a mere pretext
Violent deaths recur by gunfire assaults
For a fistful of food, people scramble
Betwixt the cries of thirst and hunger

The flowers of spring are torn apart
The dreams of the young seem upset
Tomorrow lurks behind the dawn of death
Cannot we co-exist with total faith?

HUMILIATION

When I was flourishing with youth,
When I was thriving with riches
Engaged was I with immeasurable mirth
Which slowly faded without trace.

When in joy, the whole lot stood behind
The same abandoned, when age eclipsed
Left to own fate, I am ignored and isolated
After bequeathing riches to my dear ones.

If trust and affection get betrayed by riches
If the profuse love get trampled by wealth
Can the evaporating spirit rest in peace
Unable to absorb the faltered human values.

But, when the whole world has changed
Oh God! Why should I curse my own fate?
The agonizing humiliation, I cannot bear
Yet, why still you ponder to implant a hope?

THE TRAVAILS

The rushing waves
The ravaging tides
Storm the heart
Stirring a havoc
To wreck my future
Yet another time.

The travails of gloom
The hassles of dejection
Encircle the heart
Flooring the rising hopes.
Endured time and again
But, am I still destined.

What if the ravaging tides?
Soften the rugged terrains
What if the rushing waves?
Sweep past the bygone storms
Now they cannot salvage
The daunting eventuality
Lurking to storm again
In the guise of an emotion
Hanging about to recur again.

HATRED

Somewhere, somehow I stumbled upon
Faking a smile "hatred" stood desperate.

Neither a friend nor a well wisher
Either an ovation or a peaceful shelter
Yet with ominous plans it opts to target
Who's there to share its evil-fed thought.

Bereft of love, midst a mirage of oasis
Who can comfort those who are at sea
Opulence tempts it but solitude shatters
In quest of a companion, often it bothers.

Though, to shower affection it intends
Who's there to trust it and its past deeds
The wicked repute so easily cannot erase
Most likely it sticks till the life's last phase.

From a distant view, life sparkles wonderful
It's a spider's web, luring by all the thrills
Behind the veil of illusions and disillusions
One can only seek for past revivifications.

While life disappear into the time's spindle
The soul "Hatred" tries to gulp its own finale.

THROW SOME LIGHT

When the day dawns
It brings in a bit of gloom
The beautiful nature
Though surround in rapture
I lack the instinct
To acknowledge its stint.

Around me are the paths
Thorny, devoid of any faiths
The vision ahead is totally dark
Devoid of any hope, even a spark.
Yes, the suffering people are lot
Is humanity ignored or driven out?

You love a beautiful flower
You love a drizzle of shower
While a co-human is disease stuck
Lying at the death-bed, bone suck
He is imagined ugly and vulnerable
Whose pitiable state, of course is palpable.

Starved; those who die on the streets
Unmerciful to take care of by any heart
Are thrown to the vultures of fate
Midst the human tendencies of hate.
No change is perceptible as yet ….
Upon whom we can throw some light
The dawn will actually dawn then
When, even the nature loves our nature.

EVER-NEW SOLACE

When the winds of peace
Lure us with everlasting solace,
The clouds dance to the winds
From worldly affairs, mind rewinds.
How beautiful looks the nature
How lustrous reflects our future,
In the skies, hover peace pigeons
Hopes awake in hearts horizons.

With love and concern towards all
Life looks meaningful and bountiful,
The wondrous peace replaces all foes
Melting egoism, it drives away all woes.
Eternal peace, if attained today
An unalloyed joy dawns every day
Even the noble, ordinary and the poor
Can share the shelter with equal fervor.

Blessed would be the world of peace
A marvel shall remain that storehouse;
Where, virtue reigns, illusions vanish
And dawns eternal peace, in a flash.
Unfolding a golden era of winsome
Bliss supreme shall sway our bosom;
The ocean of kindness dwells in heart
Giving ever-new solace and comfort.

MIDST AN EXILE

For a temporary but routine exile
The sleeping darkness dissolves
The morning radiance enters
Jolting the lazy nightlong thoughts.

From darkness to total light
From thoughts exile to new delights
The new rapture, of course is temporary
Yet, relentless thoughts invade memory.

We all revel at the onset of a new dawn
The wealth and richness of nature lay open
Brightness at present, darkness way behind
In rotation they keep on marching ahead.

The eager mind gallops for the elusive
Restless, aspiring to know something more
Yes, carving for something without respite
What could it be? Is it a bondage in self-exile.

A POETS' HEART

A prisoner of thoughts is every poet's heart
Where recurring thoughts pounce on the poet;
Any thought, yes, can easily stroke the poet,
And any eventuality can easily move the poet.

Midst the unison of different poetic thoughts
The poet still feels isolated with a new thirst;
But staying afloat in the vortex of new themes
He struggles for an ultimate theme and rhyme.

Autumn leaves flutter with the morning gales
Dewdrops twinkle under the tepid sunrays,
The horizon adorned with birds looks beautiful
Alluring and cool, a new season dawns gentle.

Inexplicably, a surge of musings stream out
Being a poet, I feel imprisoned in own fort;
May be yet another theme sprouts out of a seed
Before the present one hastens out to succeed.